The Ultimate IT Support Survival Guide

Proven Tips, Tools, and Techniques for Help Desk
Success

Introduction

Welcome to The Ultimate IT Support Survival Guide, crafted so anyone—from a curious retiree with a new laptop, to a teen with a MacBook for high school, or a small-business owner managing their own systems can follow along. Whether you're new to technology or have been around computers for years, this guide provides practical tips, relatable stories, and fundamental IT concepts spanning hardware, software, networking, security, data backup, and more.

Chapter 1: The Mindset of a Great IT Support Technician

Why a 'Mindset' Matters: IT support isn't just about fixing machines; it's about staying composed under pressure, listening to concerns, and viewing every problem as a puzzle—because even "simple" issues can hide surprising complexities.

1. Patience and Professionalism

Why It Matters
Tech mishaps often strike at the worst moments—like right before an important video call or when you're rushing to submit homework. Users (or you, if troubleshooting your own system) can feel overwhelmed. Remaining calm, empathetic, and friendly helps everyone stay focused on a solution.

Practical Tip
Treat every complaint—like repeated password resets or sporadic Wi-Fi drops—as though it's brand new. A patient and professional approach reassures people that they're being heard.

2. Effective Communication

Why It Matters
Many people don't speak "tech." Using too much jargon or omitting steps can confuse them and prolong the fix.

Practical Tip
Use analogies. If your computer's memory is "full," picture a desk so cluttered with papers there's no space for anything else.

3. Problem-Solving Attitude

Why It Matters
Every IT issue involves piecing together clues. Gathering facts, testing potential fixes, and documenting your results speeds resolution.

Practical Tip
Maintain a personal "fix list" of solutions you've used before. Patterns will emerge, and you'll solve repeated problems more quickly.

4. The Power of Documentation
In 1979, a faulty cooling valve at the Three Mile Island nuclear plant nearly led to a catastrophic meltdown. Engineers relied on meticulously kept logs to trace the issue and prevent disaster. Whether in nuclear safety or IT, documentation isn't just paperwork—it's the difference between chaos and control.

Takeaway: Just like those engineers used detailed logs to prevent disaster, keeping thorough documentation in IT ensures quick troubleshooting, prevents costly mistakes, and maintains system stability.

Why Documentation Matters:
- Whether you're troubleshooting for yourself or others, clear documentation helps retrace steps and find solutions faster.
- IT professionals rely on documentation to solve recurring problems and prevent mistakes.
- Even personal notes can help—if you solve an issue today, you might face it again months later.

Clear notes help avoid confusion, mitigate security risks, and show who did what.

Real-World Example

At a former workplace, we required a screenshot of a push notification as proof that a user verified themselves before unlocking their account or changing their password. One day, I verified the user successfully but forgot to attach the screenshot. Without proof, it could have been seen as granting access to an unverified user, which would have been a security breach.

Takeaway

Double-check your notes, attachments, or verification steps. A rushed process can open the door to accidents.

5. What to Do When You're Stuck

Stay Calm & Take a Short Break

Stress narrows your view; a brief pause and a deep breath or two can reveal obvious fixes.

Check the Basics

Power cables, Wi-Fi toggles, or user permissions can mimic bigger problems.

Search Effectively

Put error codes in quotes when searching online (like "Windows 10 error 0x80070057 fix") and add words like "solution" or "troubleshoot" to refine results. Searching with quotes forces search engines to find the exact phrase rather than breaking it into separate keywords, reducing irrelevant results.

Another overlooked trick is using the minus (-) operator to exclude unwanted results. For example, searching (Windows update error -reddit) removes Reddit posts from results, helping you find official MS sources faster.

Ask for Help

Who to Ask for Help:
- Small Business Owners & Individuals: Look for IT forums (Reddit's has r/techsupport, Microsoft has lots of forums, Apple has Support) or

reach out to a trusted IT consultant.
- Companies with IT Teams: If you have in-house IT, provide clear documentation when requesting help.
- Escalation: If a solution isn't working, reach out to the device manufacturer, ISP(internet service provider), or the application software provider for official support.

Be Transparent
 If you're helping someone else, let them know if you need more time. Openness reduces anxiety

Chapter 2: Troubleshooting 101 – Tools, Techniques, and Real-World Examples

In the early 1900s, "trouble shooters" literally walked along telegraph or telephone lines to find breaks. Today, troubleshooting keeps that same spirit: you isolate the issue bit by bit until you identify (and fix) it—often starting with quick checks, like verifying cables or rebooting.

Command Lines: Windows & macOS

Command Prompt (Windows) and Terminal (macOS) are text-based interfaces for controlling your system:

What is Command Line?
Instead of using a mouse to click through menus the command line allows you to type instructions directly to your system.
Think of it as talking to your computer in its native language—sometimes, it's faster and more powerful than an application's tools. And if an application is unresponsive, the command line can terminate it.

Benefits of Command Line:
- Efficiency: Tasks like checking network settings or shutting down can

be done instantly with a single command.
- Troubleshooting: Error messages often give more details than clicking buttons in Windows or macOS.
- Automation: Many IT professionals use scripts to run multiple commands at once, saving time.

Windows: Press Win + R, type cmd, press Enter, or search "cmd" in the Start menu.

macOS: Press Cmd + Space, type "Terminal," press Enter, or go to Applications → Utilities → Terminal.

Why Bother? One typed command can sometimes do what might take many clicks in a graphical interface. Plus, command lines often provide detailed feedback that helps diagnose issues more precisely.

1. The "Golden Rule" of Troubleshooting

Start Simple Many "major" problems vanish after a reboot, cable check, or short pause for the system to catch up.

Short Story: "Who's in Charge?"

Early one morning, while installing new software at a local hospital, my team got a frantic call from Lisa, a healthcare manager. She'd just gotten a new monitor and plugged it into her PC—no signal. She figured maybe the monitor was bad and tried reverting to her old one—still nothing. She even unplugged her PC at one point, reconnected cables, and got nowhere. Panicking, she called IT

The Twist: The surge protector powering her PC was completely unplugged. No monitor would ever show anything.

Extended Note: Much like the telegraph "trouble shooters," Lisa skipped the simplest check: verifying the power source.

Takeaway: Under stress, we overlook obvious fixes—always confirm power, cables, and toggles first.

2. Common Issues and Fixes

Computer Running Slowly

Windows: Press Ctrl + Shift + Esc to open Task Manager; check for an app hogging CPU/RAM. If you see unknown programs, right-click to end them. You can also disable unneeded startup apps under "Startup Apps." if you can't find that you can search for it

macOS: Click Spotlight (magnifying glass) → "Activity Monitor" to see if one app devours CPU or memory. Alternatively, to speed up boot times on a Mac, disable unnecessary startup apps by going to Apple Menu > System Settings > General > Login Items, then selecting and removing apps you don't need. Next, check Users & Groups > Login Items for hidden background processes and disable any unnecessary ones. Restart your Mac to apply the changes and enjoy a faster startup.

Printer Not Responding?

Check Connections: Are the USB cables or the Wi-Fi signal stable? Is the printer plugged into a reliable power source? A faulty extension cord can derail everything.

Windows: If print jobs are stuck, open Command Prompt (Win + R → cmd), then:
 net stop spooler

net start spooler

This restarts the "print spooler" service, which processes print tasks.

macOS: Go to System Settings → Printers & Scanners, pick your printer, and clear any stuck jobs.

Why This Helps: A jammed queue/spooler can block new print requests.

PC or Mac Won't Boot After an Update

Windows:
1. Hold Shift while clicking Restart from the Start menu.

2. Select Troubleshoot > Advanced options > Startup Settings.

3. Click Restart, then choose Safe Mode (usually option 4 or 5).

4. Go to Settings > Windows Update > Update history, uninstall the problematic update.

macOS:
1. Hold Shift immediately after pressing the power button.

2. Release when you see the Apple logo → this boots into Safe Mode.

3. Go to System Settings > Applications > Remove troublesome software.

4. Open Disk Utility (Applications > Utilities) and run First Aid to check for disk errors.

5. Restart normally to apply changes.

3. Essential Commands (Windows & macOS)

Here are basic commands that help any budding IT enthusiast solve daily problems:

Networking

Windows:
ipconfig /all – Displays detailed network information, including your IP address, internet provider, and DNS servers.

ping <IP address> – Sends small data packets to a remote address to measure round-trip time in milliseconds (ms).

Definition of Ping: Think of "ping" as a digital knock on another device. You send a small "Are you there?" request, and the device replies. The measured time (min, max, average) helps identify network slowdowns or connectivity issues.

netstat -ano – Displays active connections and ports, along with the Process ID (PID) of each connection.

ifconfig – Displays detailed network configuration and active interfaces.

ping <address> – Sends test packets to a remote device to check connectivity.

netstat -an – Shows active network connections and listening ports.

Shut Down / Restart

Windows:

shutdown /r /t 0 – Restarts the PC immediately (Restart Time=0 for PC speak).

macOS:

sudo shutdown -r now – Restarts the Mac instantly with admin privileges.

What is "sudo"? The sudo command stands for Super User Do, which grants administrator-level access. Only IT professionals or system owners should use it, as it can affect the entire system.

Process Management

Windows:

taskkill /IM processname.exe /F – Forcefully ends a process by name.

Finding the Process Name:

Open Task Manager (Ctrl + Shift + Esc) and check the Processes tab.

Some processes include the ".exe" extension, while others may not.

Run tasklist in Command Prompt to list all active processes and find the exact name.

What if the name doesn't work? Kill by PID instead:

Run tasklist to find the Process ID (PID).

Use taskkill /PID <pidnumber> /F to forcefully end the process.

macOS:
killall [process] – Ends a running process by name.

kill [PID] – Ends a process using its Process ID. Find the PID using ps aux or Activity Monitor.

System Information

Windows:
systeminfo – Displays detailed OS version and hardware specifications.

wmic os get Caption,Version – Shows the Windows version for troubleshooting or compatibility checks.

macOS:
sw_vers – Displays basic OS version information.

system_profiler – Shows a detailed report of hardware and software components.

4. Lesser-Known Tips & Tricks (Windows & macOS)

Shift + Right-Click on a folder → "Open PowerShell window here." Saves time typing paths.

Win + Shift + S → quickly capture a screenshot of a chosen area.

GodMode Folder → Create a new folder and name it:

GodMode.{ED7BA470-8E54-465E-825C-99712043E01C}

This unlocks a hidden control panel with hundreds of advanced system settings all in one place—many of which are buried deep in Windows.

Why Use It?

Instead of digging through menus, GodMode puts everything in one spot:

User accounts & admin tools, Performance tweaks, Power settings, Security options all in one location

Think of it as Windows' "cheat sheet"

Alt + Space + M → move a hidden/frozen window onto your screen if it's stuck off-display.

macOS:

Option + Click Wi-Fi → reveals extended network info (RSSI, channel, etc.).

Cmd + Shift + 4 → screenshot a region; press Space to capture a single window.

Option + Click certain icons → hidden or extra system settings.

Cmd + Ctrl + Q → lock your Mac right away.

5. Real-World Scenario: "PC Won't Boot After an Update"

Gather Info Did Windows/macOS install an update or a driver recently?

Basic Steps Use Safe Mode (Windows) or Safe Boot (macOS) to roll back or remove the culprit.

Advanced Checks

Windows: sfc /scannow (checks system file integrity), chkdsk /r (scans hard drive for errors).

macOS: Disk Utility → First Aid (press Cmd + R during boot).

Escalation Suspect hardware issues (like failing RAM or a bad HDD)? You might need replacements. This is where we'd need to pull up that part list. for ram you don't want to exceed your motherboard's speed however this is likely to undamage the ram it just will run at a lower speed. it's also best to buy sticks that have the same speed otherwise your pc will just use the slowest speed for both.

Chapter 3: Working with Users & Knowing Your Limits

IT support also involves managing emotions—both yours and the user's. Good communication plus realistic timelines can be just as crucial as technical skills.

1. Setting Expectations

Give a Time Estimate Even a rough guess ("I'll check back in 20 minutes") eases tension more than silence.

Follow Up If the fix isn't immediate, update them so they know you're still working on it.

2. Escalation and Ownership

Document Everything Log screenshots, error codes, steps you tried—someone else can step in seamlessly if needed.

Own Up to Uncertainty It's fine to say "I'm not sure," but outline how you'll investigate or escalate.

Short Story: "Morning Meltdown"

Marcus was a help desk tech who got a 7:00 AM call from an official away from the office, about to miss a Zoom meeting in 20 minutes. Marcus recalled he'd previously toggled some network settings the last time the official traveled, including Airplane Mode.

Marcus's Calm Approach: He asked if Airplane Mode was still enabled. It was—one click restored Wi-Fi, and the meeting was saved.

Takeaway: Sometimes the simplest toggles remain overlooked in a rush.

Real-World Scenario: "Email Not Sending"

Check the Basics "Did you recently change your email password?" "Are you sure you're online?"

Inspect the Client Confirm the spelling of the recipient's email address, and verify your SMTP (Simple Mail Transfer Protocol) or IMAP (Internet Message Access Protocol) settings for typos—these protocols control email sending/receiving.

SMTP (Sending): Moves emails from your device to an outgoing mail server.

IMAP (Receiving): Syncs emails with the mail server, so you see the same inbox across devices.

Search for Error Codes

Outlook: e.g., 0x800CCC0E → try "Outlook error 0x800CCC0E fix."

Apple Mail: "Outgoing server error" → "Apple Mail outgoing server error fix."

And of course search to see if anyone else is having these issues a lot of times you won't be alone

In situations like this you may need to reach out to support and escalate it. If you're working with a regular user and can't solve it, contact the company you're trying to email or their email provider (like Gmail, Yahoo, or your ISP). They may have server-side fixes or logs that can help.

Chapter 4: Advanced Networking

Networking is the nervous system of computing, linking devices, servers, and entire offices to share data. From small home Wi-Fi setups to multi-office corporate LANs, well-planned networks keep data flowing smoothly.

Fascinating Networking Story: In 1969, UCLA attempted to connect to Stanford using ARPANET—an early version of the internet (a WAN, or Wide Area Network). They only managed to send the "LO" part of "LOGIN" before crashing, but that "LO" proved data could traverse hundreds of miles between two distant computers.

Additional Network Types

WAN: Wide Area Network, covering large geographical regions/cities.

LAN: Local Area Network, for homes/offices.

PAN: Personal Area Network, like a Bluetooth setup around a single person.

1. VLANs, Subnets, and IP Addressing

VLANs, Subnets, and IP Addressing Explained

In networking, devices communicate using IP addresses, just like buildings have street addresses. But to keep networks organized, efficient, and secure, we use tools like VLANs, subnets, and different IP address types.

VLAN: Virtual LAN (Local Area Network)

A VLAN is like creating separate private sections within the same building without building physical walls.

Think of a large office space with marketing, sales, and IT departments all working in one big open floor. If they all used the same shared network, it could become overloaded and unsecure.

Instead, with VLANs, the company can logically separate the departments, even though they are still physically in the same building. IT can have it's own VLAN, separate from Marketing, so that their traffic doesn't interfere with each other.

Switches are devices that manage VLANs—imagine them as security guards directing people to their assigned floors.

Subnets: Dividing Networks for Performance & Security

A subnet (short for subnetwork) helps break a large network into smaller, more manageable pieces.

If an entire college campus had every student on one big network, it would be slow and chaotic.

By subnetting, they could separate students, faculty, and guests, improving speed and adding security controls.

Each subnet acts like separate wings in a hospital—ER, Surgery, Pediatrics—they are all part of the same hospital but have separate areas for efficiency.

DHCP: Dynamic Host Configuration Protocol

DHCP automatically assigns IP addresses to devices so users don't have to do it manually.

Imagine renting a car—you don't keep the same car every time; you're assigned a different one when needed.

Similarly, DHCP dynamically gives devices an available IP address when they connect to the network.

Without DHCP, you'd have to manually configure every device, which is inefficient.

Static IP: A Fixed Address for Servers,Printers, security systems.

A static IP is a permanent address for devices that should always be found in the same place—like a VIP reserved parking spot.

Good for devices like servers, network printers, and security cameras that need a consistent location to function properly.

The Apartment Analogy: How IP Addresses Work

An IP address is like a building address in a city.

Each device (computer, phone, printer) is like an apartment inside that building, with it's own unique unit number.

Just like two apartments can't have the same number, two devices on the same network can't have the same IP address—or else network conflicts occur (like getting mail meant for someone else).

Why We Needed IPv6 (and How Long Until We Run Out)

IPv4 (Internet Protocol version 4) was created in the 1980s and uses 32-bit numbers, which allowed for about 4.3 billion addresses. That seemed like a lot at that time before the internet exploded, but with billions of people and devices online, we started running out of IPv4 addresses quickly.

To solve this, ISPs (Internet Service Providers) had to get creative by using sub-IP addresses (like NAT – Network Address Translation) to share one public IPv4 address among multiple devices.

NAT: Network Address Translation, letting many private IPs hide behind one public IP.

IPv6: The New Standard

IPv6 uses 128-bit addresses, which allows for 340 undecillion (340 trillion trillion trillion) addresses—enough to assign an IP address to every grain of sand on Earth, millions of times over.

Why the mix of letters and numbers? Unlike IPv4, which only used numbers, IPv6 includes both letters (A-F) and numbers (0-9), making it exponentially larger.

How long will it last? If IPv4 ran out in about 30 years, IPv6 is expected to last for hundreds of years, if not forever due to its massive scale.

Key Differences: IPv4 vs IPv6

IPv4: 32-bit numeric (e.g., 111.111.111.111), nearly depleted.

IPv6: 128-bit alphanumeric (e.g., 2001:0db8:85a3:0000:0000:8a2e:0370:7334), ensuring a vast address pool.

Short Story: "My First Home Network"

When I set up my first home network, I wanted to create a 'smart' setup with static IPs, a game server, and multiple Wi-Fi channels. What could go wrong?
- I accidentally assigned the same static IP to my laptop and gaming PC, making them 'compete' for the connection—knocking each other offline.
- My 'separate Wi-Fi channels' plan backfired when my router split devices onto different networks, preventing my printer from connecting.

I can't tell you the level of frustration I had—for days... actual days.
- Finally, I set up DHCP properly, assigned correct static IPs, and restored network sanity.

Takeaway: Even a home network can get complicated fast—good planning and troubleshooting skills go a long way!

2. DNS Basics

DNS: Domain Name System, which translates friendly names (like google.com) into numeric IP addresses. Like googles 8.8.8.8 that i often use for network speed tests

Common DNS Issues: stale caches, misconfigured DNS servers, blocked domains.
What These Issues Mean:
- Stale Cache: Your system stores old DNS records, causing incorrect routing. Fix it with:
  - Windows: `ipconfig /flushdns`
  - Mac: `sudo killall -HUP mDNSResponder`
- Blocked Domains: Some websites may be restricted by your ISP, firewall, or security settings.
  - Check if your network administrator or security software is blocking the site.
  - Try switching to Google's DNS (`8.8.8.8`) or Cloudflare's DNS (`1.1.1.1`) to bypass bad ISP settings.

Check DNS:
Windows: nslookup google.com, ipconfig /flushdns

macOS: dig google.com, sudo killall -HUP mDNSResponder

3. Network Troubleshooting Commands

tracert [IP address] – short for "trace route," this command shows each "hop" data takes across routers to reach its destination. Each hop represents a step along the way: the first hop is typically your device, the next is your router, followed by your internet provider's network, then various backbone servers, until it reaches the final destination, like Google's server at 8.8.8.8. This helps diagnose network slowdowns by revealing where delays or failures occur.

netsh int ip reset: Resets the TCP/IP stack, which can fix network-related issues on Windows.

traceroute [IP Address]: Mac's version of tracert, showing the path data takes to its destination.

networksetup -listallhardwareports: Lists all network interfaces on a Mac, helping identify which one is in use.

sudo ifconfig en0 down && sudo ifconfig en0 up: Resets the network interface "en0" on a Mac, often used for troubleshooting connection issues.

Real-World Scenario: "Users on One VLAN Can't Access the Internet"

First Steps to Troubleshoot:

Check VLAN Configuration: Ensure the VLAN is properly tagged on the switch. If it's misconfigured, devices may not communicate properly.

Verify Gateway Settings: Each device should have the correct default gateway assigned to route traffic outside its VLAN.

Check DNS or Firewall Rules: If internet access is blocked, verify that DNS settings are correct and that firewall rules aren't preventing that VLAN from accessing the web.

Try Basic Network Resets:

On Windows, use netsh int ip reset to refresh network settings.

On Mac, use sudo ifconfig en0 down && sudo ifconfig en0 up to restart the network interface.

Run a Network Trace:

Use tracert [IP] on Windows or traceroute [IP] on Mac to check where the connection is failing.

If You Can't Fix It Alone: Escalate to your network admin or ISP to determine if the issue is outside your control. Which does happen more often than you'd think, especially with remote workers, sometimes we are aware of an outage at the same time as the isps.

Chapter 5: Security Basics

Security protects data and systems from unauthorized access. Whether it's your personal laptop or a business network, solid security habits are crucial.

Why Security Matters:

One breach (like ransomware or phishing) can destroy family photos, homework assignments, or entire business records. Recovery costs and lost trust can be huge.

1. Recognizing Phishing, AI Scams & Social Engineering

Advanced Email Scam Detection Tricks:
- Check the sender email: A scammer might use `george34532@random.com` instead of an official business email.
- Hover over links: Without clicking, hover over any links to see if they redirect to a suspicious website.
- Look for urgency tactics: Scammers often use phrases like 'Immediate Action Required!' to rush you.
- Verify with the real company: If an email seems suspicious, call the company's official number instead of using the email's links.

Look for Red Flags: suspicious email addresses, urgent "click now" links, odd attachments.

And AI can mimic voices/writing styles now, so trust your instincts if something feels off.

Verify Before Acting: if something's suspicious, look at the email details? who sent it-often times phishing users will have a simple name with letters and numbers following it like above. if it's from a legitimate business you can research the business and potentially the email itself remember to use quotes when you want to see that specifically. And Double-check phone calls that seem "weird," as AI can clone voices now.

2. Password Management

Use MFA: Multi-Factor Authentication can be a text code you recieve on your phone, an authenticator app, or biometrics (fingerprint, face ID). This drastically reduces hack success, as it's much harder for someone to gain access using a secure password versus a typical "123456" combo.

And please—never use a basic password like that.

The best password you can have is a randomly generated mix of letters, numbers, and symbols"Smashing your hand on the keyboard," as my instructor used to say.

But keep that stored in a password manager to remember for you.

If that's not an option, using a long passphrase has also been shown to take centuries to crack.

Example: "ShellysDressWasWhiteWhenWeMetIn2006"

How Long It Takes to Crack a Password

6-character password (lowercase only) → Instant

8-character password (mixed case + numbers) → 8 hours

10-character password (mixed case + numbers + symbols) → 5 years

12-character password (full complexity) → 300 years

16-character password (full complexity) → Millions of years

The longer and more complex your password, the harder it is to crack. Using a password manager ensures you can use long, unique passwords without forgetting them.

Never Store Passwords in Plain Text: If attackers see it, your account is theirs. Keep them out of sight—no sticky notes on your desk!

Use password managers like Bitwarden or 1Password, and consider enabling BitLocker on Windows (linked to your Microsoft account) for full disk encryption. If you ever suspect a password is exposed, change it immediately and/or notify IT.

3. Company Policy & Compliance

Data Handling: If you manage health data, follow HIPAA. If you deal with payments, check PCI-DSS. If you have EU personal data, look at GDPR.

Device Security: Laptops with FileVault (macOS) or BitLocker (Windows) are safer if stolen.

Real-World Scenario: "Hacker with a Stolen Identity"

In 2015, a security consultant tested a major data center by posing as a high-level executive with a stolen staff ID. He got to the front desk to give him a tour and once he got there he called from inside the server room, demonstrating how easily he'd gained physical access. And from there he nearly accessed crucial data.

Takeaway: Physical security is often the weakest link—verifying IDs is just as important as digital encryption.

Real-World Scenario: "Suspicious Logins Detected"

Check Access Logs: local vs. foreign IP? malicious region?

Alert the User: force a password reset if attempts persist.

Escalate: multiple compromised accounts hint at a bigger breach.

Remote Work Security Policies for Small Businesses

- Require VPN usage: Encrypts employee traffic and prevents public Wi-Fi attacks.

- Enable Multi-Factor Authentication (MFA): Reduces risk of account breaches.

- Use endpoint protection software: Helps detect malware on remote devices.

- Set up automatic updates: Ensures that all software is up-to-date with security patches.

- Create clear IT policies: Define guidelines on device usage, file sharing, and remote access.

Chapter 6: Automation & Scripting

In IT, time is precious. Automation—through scripts or specialized tools—turns tedious, repetitive tasks into quick, error-resistant operations, letting you focus on bigger issues.

Opening Anecdote

When I started out, I manually created user accounts whenever new hires arrived—a time-consuming chore. A colleague showed me PowerShell scripts, and suddenly, that multi-step process collapsed into one command. I realized automation frees you from drudge work.

1. PowerShell Essentials (Windows)

What Is PowerShell? A more advanced command-line environment integrated with .NET, offering object-oriented scripting capabilities that surpass traditional Command Prompt.

Cmdlets: specialized commands built into PowerShell (short for "command-lets").

Get-Help [cmdlet]: usage/examples.

Accessing PowerShell: Press Win + R, type powershell, hit Enter, or search "PowerShell."

Basic Automation Example (Windows)

Example: Automated Cleanup Script

Stops Print Spooler, removes temp files, restarts Spooler.

$Service = "Spooler"

Stop-Service $Service -Force

Remove-Item -Path "C:\Windows\Temp*" -Recurse -Force

Start-Service $Service

Write-Host "Cleanup complete!"

2. macOS Shell & Automator

Terminal Scripts (.sh): schedule backups, gather logs, or run updates (sudo softwareupdate -ia).

Automator: a drag-and-drop workflow builder for tasks like file renaming, photo resizing, etc.

Real-World Scenario: "Mass Password Reset"

PowerShell (Windows Domain): loop through a CSV of Active Directory users, resetting passwords.

Logging: store output for audit/compliance.

Verification: confirm each account updated, require a password change on next login.

Short Story: "Hospital Lobby Insight"

I once set up a laptop for a surgeon in a hectic hospital lobby. A somewhat graphic plastic surgery reality show played overhead. The surgeon hardly looked up, shrugging, "That's not too complicated," while I changed his laptop's resolution—a tiny fix for me, but vital for his telehealth consultations.

Takeaway: Small tech tweaks on your end can be enormous for someone else's workflow.

Chapter 7: Cloud & Virtualization

"The cloud" revolutionized data hosting and services by removing reliance on local hardware, while virtualization lets multiple "computers" (VMs) run safely on a single physical machine.

Why the Cloud Changed the World

Before cloud computing, companies had to buy and maintain all their own servers, limiting growth and budget. Now, a tiny startup can become global in minutes, and big corporations scale or shrink at will.

1. Virtual Machines (VMs)

Why VMs?: test software without risking your main OS, or run multiple OSes on one machine. If the VM crashes, your host stays safe.

Common Platforms: VMware, Hyper-V, VirtualBox.

Snapshots: "save points" you can revert to if an update/installation fails.

2. Cloud Services

Major Providers: AWS, Microsoft Azure, Google Cloud.

Origins: though "time-sharing" concepts trace to the 1960s, modern cloud soared in the mid-2000s with AWS.

Common Pitfalls: misconfigured security groups, minimal permissions, or poor connectivity hamper performance.

Real-World Scenario: "VM Running Slowly"

Resource Check: ensure enough CPU/RAM, check if the virtual disk is near capacity.

Hypervisor Logs: repeated errors can indicate deeper issues.

Network Throughput: bandwidth or firewall constraints might throttle speed.

Chapter 8: Data Backup & Recovery

Data is at the core of everything: cherished photos, vital homework, critical business records. Losing data to hardware crashes, ransomware, or a coffee spill can be devastating.

Picture discovering your laptop's hard drive is wrecked or your primary server is corrupt beyond repair, and you lack backups. Years of work or memories—gone. A robust backup plan turns catastrophe into a minor inconvenience.

Local vs. Cloud Backups

Local: external drives or a NAS for quick offline access, but vulnerable to local disasters (fires, floods, theft).

Cloud: OneDrive, Google Drive, Dropbox—offsite redundancy, often with versioning to revert corrupted/encrypted files.

Offline/Cold Backups: physically disconnected drives remain safe from malware.

Real-World Story: "The Server Flood"

A small accounting firm stored everything on an in-office server and did daily backups on another machine in the same room. A burst pipe destroyed both, erasing years of financial data.

Takeaway: offsite or cloud backups can save you from location-based disasters.

Ransomware Readiness

Versioned Cloud Storage: revert to earlier file versions if encryption hit's.

Testing Restores: retrieve at least one file monthly to confirm backups actually work.

Simple Ways to Back Up Data

External Drive: copy crucial folders weekly, keep the drive away from your main computer (in a safe or another room).

Cloud Sync: auto-sync a folder (OneDrive, Google Drive, etc.) for important docs.

Imaging Software: Macrium Reflect, Acronis True Image for full disk images.

Appendix: Quick Reference & Buying Guide

A. Quick Reference Checklists

Ch. 1: empathize, document thoroughly, escalate if needed.

Ch. 2: start simple, define ping and spooler, check for stuck queues.

Ch. 3: give time estimates, own uncertainty, manage user stress.

Ch. 4: VLANs/subnets help networks, watch DNS/firewalls, escalate to net admin if stuck.

Ch. 5: suspect phishing/AI scams, use MFA, keep physical security tight, never store passwords in plain sight.

Ch. 6: automate repetitive tasks (PowerShell, Automator), keep logs, note that PowerShell is an advanced CLI.

Ch. 7: the cloud freed us from local servers, VMs isolate your main OS, watch misconfigs.

Ch. 8: local + cloud backups, test restores, plan for disasters.

Maintenance Checklists (Weekly/Monthly)

Weekly:

Install OS/security updates.

Empty Recycle Bin/Trash.

Confirm antivirus definitions (latest virus info).

Check backups for errors.

Monthly:

Clear temp files/logs.

Update major software (browsers, plugins, etc.).

Test-restore a file from backup.

Review user permissions.

Basic Troubleshooting Flowchart:

Computer won't power on?

Check cables & surge protector

Try another device in same outlet

No? → possibly a bad outlet

Yes? → check the computer's power supply or battery

Escalate if still unresolved

B. Basic Hardware & Software Buying Guidance

Essential Specs:

RAM: ideally 2 sticks for dual-channel (e.g., 2×8 GB for 16 GB). Dual-channel is faster than a single stick. 8 GB is no longer recommended and should only be used for very light tasks; 16 GB is more comfortable now.

CPU: Intel i5/i7/i9 or AMD Ryzen 5/7 for typical use. Higher tiers (i9, Ryzen 9) handle heavy gaming/editing.

Storage: an SSD (256–512 GB). M.2 NVMe drives are faster than older SATA SSDs. Windows/macOS can use up 30 GB+, so 512 GB if you store lots of data.

Peripherals: a reliable router (e.g., TP-Link Archer), an external backup drive, and a decent printer.

Windows vs. macOS:

Windows (by Microsoft, 1975, Bill Gates & Paul Allen): widely used, broad compatibility, range of price points.

macOS (by Apple, 1976, Steve Jobs/Wozniak/Wayne): tight hardware/software integration, often pricier, known for design and updates.

C. Budget-Conscious Software Recommendations

Antivirus/Antimalware: Windows Defender (built-in, free), Malwarebytes (free scans, paid real-time).

Password Managers: Bitwarden (great free tier), 1Password (paid).

Productivity Tools: Microsoft 365 vs. Google Workspace; free options like LibreOffice.

Automation: Zapier, IFTTT, or OS schedulers (Task Scheduler on Windows, Cron on macOS/Linux).

Conclusion & Final Tips:

Final Takeaways for Everyone:
- For Beginners: Focus on learning troubleshooting basics—checking power, restarting, and documenting fixes.
- For Small Businesses: Set up a solid security policy, automate backups, and keep track of IT issues.
- For Advanced Users: Experiment with scripting and automation—PowerShell, Linux bash scripts, and Python can make IT work easier.
- For Everyone: Always stay curious! The more you explore IT, the more confident you'll become in solving problems.

Becoming an excellent IT support technician (or just a savvy computer user) demands technical skill, empathetic communication, and constant learning. Each fix—whether for a meltdown, system upgrade, or server glitch—enhances your expertise.

Advice from Professionals

Stay Curious: tech evolves constantly—explore and keep learning

Document Everything: logs, screenshots, knowledge bases minimize confusion.

Prioritize Security: small oversights can lead to big breaches.

Network with Others: IT forums, conferences, local meetups—peer insights broaden your perspective.

Find a Starting Point: help desk or entry-level support can lead to systems administration, cybersecurity, or cloud engineering.

Remember: The fundamentals here serve you throughout your IT journey. Keep learning, embrace challenges, and enjoy the ever-changing world of tech support!

Glossary of IT Terms:

AI: (Artificial Intelligence): Machines that simulate human intelligence processes.

ARPANET: Early network from the 1960s that led to the modern internet.

BIOS/UEFI: Basic firmware that initiates your computer's boot; UEFI is the newer standard.

CMD: Short for Command Prompt on Windows.

DHCP: Dynamic Host Configuration Protocol, auto-assigns IP addresses.

DNS: Domain Name System, resolving domain names (like example.com) to IPs.

GPU: Graphics Processing Unit, handles rendering of images/videos.

HDD/SSD: Hard Disk Drive or Solid-State Drive; types of storage media.

IP Address: A numerical label (e.g., 192.168.0.5) identifying a device on a network.

LAN/WAN/PAN: Local/Wide/Personal Area Network, describing different network scales.

MFA: Multi-Factor Authentication; adding extra security beyond just a password.

NAS: Network Attached Storage, a storage device shared over a network.

NAT: Network Address Translation, multiple private IPs sharing one public IP.

PID: Process ID, a unique identifier for a running program.

Ping: A utility sending tiny data packets to measure round-trip time, returned in ms (min, max, avg)—like a "hello" to see if a device is reachable and how quick.

SMTP/IMAP: Email protocols for sending (SMTP) and receiving (IMAP) mail.

SSL/TLS: Encryption protocols securing data in transit.

VM: Virtual Machine, a separate "computer" running inside another.

About the Author

Ryan Nowack is an IT professional with over a decade of experience translating tech confusion into clarity. He's worked across Windows, macOS, and Linux systems, helping people navigate everything from everyday glitches to deeper system issues — all without drowning them in jargon or tech speak.

He writes guides that feel like you're getting help from a friend who actually knows what they're doing (and won't judge your 57 open browser tabs). Based in Michigan, Ryan also dabbles in digital art, tech repair, and consuming way too much coffee.

Whether you're a beginner or just tech-anxious, his goal is simple: help you get things working—and understand why they work in the first place..